1938 U.S. YEARBOOK

ISBN: 9781790458509

FIRST EDITION

PEOPLE IN HIGH OFFICE

Franklin D. Roosevelt
March 4, 1933 - April 12, 1945
Democratic Party

Born January 30, 1882 and commonly known by his initials FDR he served as the 32nd President of the United States. He died April 12, 1945.

48 stars (1912-1959)

Vice President: John Nance Garner
Chief Justice: Charles Evans Hughes
Speakers of the House of Representatives: William B. Bankhead
Senate Majority Leader: Alben W. Barkley

UNITED KINGDOM

Monarch **King George VI**	**Prime Minister** **Neville Chamberlain**

Dec 11, 1936 - Feb 6, 1952	May 28, 1937 - May 10, 1940

Australia

Canada

Ireland

Prime Minister
Joseph Lyons
United Australia Party
Jan 6, '32 - Apr 7, '39

Prime Minister
Mackenzie King
Liberal Party
Oct 23, '35 - Nov 15, '48

Taoiseach of Ireland
Éamon de Valera
Fianna Fáil
Dec 29, '37 - Feb 18, '48

REST OF THE WORLD

Argentina

Presidents
Agustín Pedro Justo
Roberto María Ortiz

Brazil

President
Getúlio Vargas

Republic Of
China

Premiers
Chiang Kai-shek
Kung Hsiang-hsi

Cuba

President
Federico Laredo Brú

France

President
Albert François Lebrun

Germany

Chancellor
Adolf Hitler

Greece

Prime Minister
Ioannis Metaxas

India

Governor General / Viceroy Of India
Victor Alexander John Hope

Italy

Prime Minister
Benito Mussolini

Japan

Prime Minister
Prince Fumimaro Konoe

Mexico

President
Lázaro Cárdenas

New Zealand

Prime Minister
Michael Joseph Savage

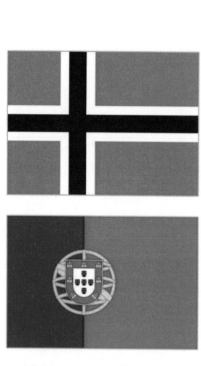

Norway

Prime Minister
Johan Nygaardsvold

Portugal

Premier
António de Oliveira Salazar

South Africa

Prime Minister
J. B. M. Hertzog

Russia

Communist Party Leader
Joseph Stalin

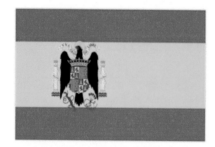

Spain

Head of State
Francisco Franco

Turkey

Prime Minister
Celâl Bayar

EVENTS FROM 1938

JANUARY

3 The March of Dimes Foundation (originally named the National Foundation for Infantile Paralysis) is established by President Franklin D. Roosevelt. Initially this non-profit organization focused on combatting polio but the foundation has since expanded this and now works to improve the health of mothers and babies.

6 A bronze memorial statue of Henry Hudson is erected in Henry Hudson Park in the Bronx, NYC. Henry Hudson is credited as the first European to have discovered the Hudson River (which is named after him).

16 The Famous 1938 Carnegie Hall Jazz Concert is recorded live with Benny Goodman and his Orchestra. This landmark recording was also the premiere performance given by a jazz orchestra in the famed Carnegie Hall in New York City.

17 Joseph P. Kennedy becomes the 44th United States Ambassador to the United Kingdom

22 Thornton Wilder's play 'Our Town' is performed for the first time in Princeton, New Jersey. It later went on to success on Broadway and won the Pulitzer Prize for Drama.

27 The Niagara Falls Bridge collapses due to an ice jam.

28 The first ski tow in America begins operation in Vermont. Located on the Charles Clark Farm the tow is 1,100 feet long.

The scene in the aftermath of the great Niagara Falls Bridge collapse.

The Niagara Falls Bridge (otherwise known as the Honeymoon Bridge) was built in 1898 by the Pencoyd Bridge Company of Philadelphia under the direction of Engineer R.S. Buck. The bridges' collapse was caused by a powerful wind storm that blew ice from Lake Erie down the Niagara River and over both the Horseshoe and the American Falls. The ice began to mount higher and higher and eventually caused the bridge to collapse at 4:20pm January 27. The bridge was replaced by the current Rainbow Bridge which was opened on November 1, 1941, just 500ft from the site of the Niagara Falls Bridge.

FEBRUARY

7   The tire manufacturer Harvey Firestone (born December 20, 1868) dies.

23   Joe Louis retains The Ring and world heavyweight titles by knocking out Nathan Mann in 3 rounds. Louis further defends his titles two more times in 1938, on April 1 against Harry Thomas and June 22 against Max Schmeling.

1: Harvey Firestone posing with car and truck tires at his Akron Plant in Ohio.
2: An early race-car advertising Firestone tires.

Harvey Firestone was one of the first global makers of automobile tires. He founded the Firestone Tire and Rubber Company in 1900 to supply pneumatic tires for wagons, buggies and other forms of wheeled transportation common in the era. Firestone soon saw the huge potential for marketing tires for automobiles and became a pioneer in their mass production. Harvey Firestone was great friends with Henry Ford and he became an original equipment supplier to Ford Motor Company automobiles.

MARCH

3   The Los Angeles floods of 1938: Pacific storms cause the Santa Ana, Los Angeles and San Gabriel rivers to burst their banks.

10   The 10th Academy Awards are held at the Biltmore Hotel in Los Angeles, California and are hosted by Bob Burns. The Life of Emile Zola (1937) takes the Best Picture Award.

1: Downtown Los Angeles - 2: William L. Griffin digs out the family car.

The Los Angeles floods were one of the most catastrophic natural disasters in Southern California history. It resulted in $40 million in damages and the deaths of 115 people.

APRIL

8	Jazz cornet player and bandleader Joe 'King' Oliver (born December 19, 1881) dies. Oliver was a mentor and teacher to Louis Armstrong.
25	The U.S. Supreme Court overturns a century of federal common law in its decision in the case of Erie Railroad Co. v. Tompkins. The Court held that federal courts did not have the judicial power to create general federal common law when hearing state law claims under diversity jurisdiction.
28	The towns of Dana, Enfield, Greenwich and Prescott are disincorporated to make way for the Quabbin Reservoir.
30	The first cartoon to feature Happy Rabbit, 'Porky's Hare Hunt', is released. Happy Rabbit was the prototype for Bugs Bunny, who had his official debut in 'A Wild Hare' in 1940.

Bugs Bunny's evolution from Happy Rabbit in 1938 to the present day.

The prototypical version of Bugs Bunny appeared in four cartoons before making his official debut in 1940. Bugs Bunny has appeared in more films than any other cartoon character and has his own star on the Hollywood Walk of Fame.

MAY

17	The radio quiz show 'Information Please' debuts on NBC. The show runs until April 22, 1951.

JUNE

18	Babe Ruth is signed as a Dodgers first base coach.
23	The Civil Aeronautics Act is signed into law forming the Civil Aeronautics Authority. Now renamed the Civil Aeronautics Board (CAB) the agency regulates aviation services and provides air accident investigation.
23	Marineland, billed as 'the world's first oceanarium', opens near St. Augustine, Florida. The admission price is $1.
24	A 496-ton meteorite explodes about 12 miles above the earth near Chicora, Pennsylvania.
25	The Food, Drug and Cosmetic Act was signed into law by president Franklin D. Roosevelt. It gives authority to the U.S. Food and Drug Administration (FDA) to oversee the safety of food, drugs and cosmetics.
30	Action Comics issue No.1 is published by DC Comics and features the first ever appearance of Superman.

The front cover of Action Comics issue No.1 featuring Superman.

Issue No.1 features the first appearance of several comic book heroes but most notably the Jerry Siegel and Joe Shuster creation, Superman. For this reason it is widely considered both the beginning of the superhero genre and the most valuable comic book of all time. On August 24, 2014, a copy graded 9.0 by CGC was sold on eBay for US$3,207,852.

1 - 4	The last reunion of the Blue and Gray commemorates the 75th anniversary of the Battle of Gettysburg in Gettysburg, Pennsylvania.
5	The Non-Intervention Committee reaches an agreement to withdraw all foreign volunteers from the Spanish Civil War. The agreement is respected by most Republican foreign volunteers, notably by those from England and the United States, but is ignored by the governments of Germany and Italy.
14	Howard Hughes sets a new record by completing a flight around the world in just 91 hours (3d 19h 17m) and beats the previous record set in 1933 by Wiley Post by almost four days.
17	Douglas Corrigan takes off from New York City heading for California in his single-engine aircraft. 28 hours later he lands his plane in Dublin Ireland.

Douglas 'Wrong Way' Corrigan alongside his rebuilt $325 1929 Curtiss Robin monoplane.

Douglas Corrigan had modified his aircraft for long flights but was repeatedly refused permission to complete a transatlantic journey. In July 1938, Corrigan piloted the single-engine plane nonstop from California to New York. Almost immediately after arriving in New York he filed plans for a transatlantic flight but aviation authorities deemed it a suicide flight and he was promptly denied. Instead they would allow Corrigan to fly back to the West Coast and on July 17 he took off from Floyd Bennett field ostentatiously pointed west. However a few minutes later he made a 180-degree turn and vanished into a cloudbank to the puzzlement of a few onlookers. Twenty-eight hours and 13 minutes later he landed at Baldonnel Airport in Dublin, Ireland. Having flown 3,150 miles, he claimed he "had been following the wrong end of the magnetic needle." Officials were skeptical, but he said, "That's my story". By the time 'Wrong Way' Corrigan and his crated plane had returned to New York by ship he was a national celebrity. New York City honoured him with a ticker-tape parade which was attended by an estimated 1 million people.

AUGUST

6	Warner Brothers release the Looney Tunes animated short Porky & Daffy.
18	The Thousand Islands Bridge (opened in 1937) connecting the United States with Canada is dedicated by President Roosevelt.
22	Two people were reported killed and more than 51 others were injured in a rear end collision between two Lexington Avenue, New York subway trains.

SEPTEMBER

1	Haggar debuts a new pant concept, 'Slacks', as the appropriate pant to wear during a man's 'Slack Time'.
4	During a ceremony in France, marking the unveiling of a plaque at Pointe de Grave celebrating Franco-American friendship, American Ambassador William Bullitt states, 'France and the United States were united in war and peace'. This leads to much speculation in the press that if war did break out over Czechoslovakia then the U.S. would join the war on the Allied side.
9	President Roosevelt disallows the popular interpretation of Bullitt's speech at a press conference at the White House. Roosevelt states it is '100% wrong' the U.S. would join a 'stop-Hitler bloc' under any circumstances and makes it quite clear that in the event of German aggression against Czechoslovakia, the U.S. would remain neutral.
15	American author Thomas Clayton Wolfe (born October 3, 1900) dies after being diagnosed with miliary tuberculosis of the brain.
21	The New England Hurricane of 1938 strikes Long Island and southern New England. It kills over 300 along the Rhode Island shoreline and approximately 600 in total.
22	Olsen and Johnson's musical comedy revue Hellzapoppin' begins its 3-year run on Broadway. It becomes one of only three plays to run more than 500 performances in the 1930s and by 1941 it was the longest-running Broadway musical with 1,404 performances.
23	A time capsule (to be opened in 6939) is buried at World's Fair in NYC. More than 100 items were placed in the capsule including a Kodak camera, a woman's hat, man's pipe, some Dr. West's tooth powder and 1,100ft of microfilm.

OCTOBER

10	The Blue Water Bridge opens connecting Port Huron, Michigan and Sarnia, Ontario.
13	Cartoonist E. C. Segar (born December 8, 1894), best known as the creator of Popeye, dies. Segar is widely regarded as one of the most influential and talented cartoonists of all time and was among the first to combine humor with long-running adventures.
16	Winston Churchill, in a broadcast address to the United States, condemns the Munich Agreement as a defeat and calls upon America and Western Europe to prepare for armed resistance against Adolf Hitler.
24	The minimum wage is established by law in the U.S. and set at $0.25 per hour.
30	Orson Welles's radio adaptation of The War of the Worlds is broadcast and reportedly causes panic in parts of the U.S.
31	In an effort to try restore investor confidence the New York Stock Exchange unveils a 15-point program intended to upgrade protection for the investing public.

OCTOBER

FAKE RADIO 'WAR' STIRS TERROR THROUGH U.S.

1: Orson Welles during his War of the Worlds broadcast.
2: The Daily News headlines the following day.

Just after 8pm on October 30, 1938 listeners to CBS Radio were treated to an unusual dramatization of H.G. Wells's classic 'The War of the Worlds' performed by 23-year-old wunderkind Orson Welles and his Mercury Theater on the Air. Although most listeners understood that the program was a radio drama the next day's headlines reported that thousands of people were plunged into panic and were convinced that America was under a deadly Martian attack. The reality of the panic is disputed as the program had relatively few listeners but the episode secured Welles's fame as a dramatist.

NOVEMBER

1   Seabiscuit defeats War Admiral by four lengths in their famous horse race at Pimlico Race Course in Baltimore, Maryland. An estimated 40 million people listened to the race around the world including President Roosevelt, who, during a cabinet meeting, stopped all business of presiding over the nation to listen to the broadcast.

10   On the eve of Armistice Day, Kate Smith sings Irving Berlin's revised version of 'God Bless America' for the first time on her weekly radio show.

15   President Roosevelt read a statement to the media strongly condemning the persecution of Jews in Germany and announcing that he had recalled the American ambassador to Germany.

DECEMBER

President Roosevelt agrees to lend $25 million to Chiang Kai-shek's government cementing the US-Chinese relationship and angering the Japanese government.

26   The Earl Carroll Theatre opens on 6230 Sunset Boulevard in Hollywood. Over the entrance Carroll emblazoned the words 'Through these portals pass the most beautiful girls in the world'.

31   The Boeing 307 Stratoliner has its first flight. The Stratoliner is the first commercial transport aircraft to enter service with a pressurized cabin allowing the aircraft to cruise at an altitude of 20,000ft. The Model 307 has capacity for a crew of six and 33 passengers.

10 NOTEABLE WORLDWIDE EVENTS

1. Peter Carl Goldmark demonstrated the first color television. The system transmitted on 343 lines (about 100 lines less than a black and white set) and at a different field scan rate so was therefore incompatible with television sets currently on the market without an adapter.
2. Albert Einstein and Leopold Infeld publish The Evolution of Physics.
3. On March 4 bio-gerontologist Raymond Pearl demonstrates the negative health effects of tobacco smoking.
4. Roy Joseph Plunkett of DuPont accidentally discovers polytetrafluoroethylene (Teflon) on April 6.
5. Berlin based Konrad Zuse completes his mechanical calculator Z1 computer. Using Boolean logic it reads instructions from perforated 35mm film.
6. The world's largest airship the Graf Zeppelin II makes maiden flight on September 14.
7. Frenchman László Bíró obtains his first patent for a ballpoint pen.
8. Captain George Eyston sets the world land speed record at 357.5mph on September 16 in his car Thunderbolt.
9. The first patents for nylon (first synthesised in 1935) are granted in the name of Wallace Carothers to DuPont. The first items produced with the new material are toothbrush bristles.
10. On October 22 physicist and lawyer Chester Carlson makes the first successful Xerox copy with his assistant Otto Kornei.

THUNDERBOLT

U.S. PERSONALITIES

BORN IN 1938

Frank A. Langella, Jr.
January 1, 1938

Stage and film actor who has won four Tony Awards for his performances as Richard Nixon in Frost/Nixon, André in The Father, Leslie in Edward Albee's Seascape and as Flegont Alexandrovitch Tropatchov in Ivan Turgenev's Fortune's Fool. Additionally, Langella has won two Obie Awards and was nominated for an Academy Award for Best Actor in a Leading Role in the film production of Frost/Nixon (2008).

Allen Toussaint
January 14, 1938 -
November 10, 2015

Musician, songwriter, arranger and record producer who was an influential figure in New Orleans R&B from the 1950s to the end of the century. Toussaint was inducted into the Rock and Roll Hall of Fame in 1998, the Louisiana Music Hall of Fame in 2009 and the Songwriter's Hall of Fame and the Blues Hall of Fame in 2011. In 2013 he was awarded the National Medal of Arts by President Barack Obama.

Curtis Charles Flood
January 18, 1938 -
January 20, 1997

Major League Baseball center fielder who spent 15-seasons in the major leagues playing for the Cincinnati Redlegs, St. Louis Cardinals and Washington Senators. Flood was an All-Star for three seasons and Gold Glove winner for seven consecutive seasons. He retired in 1971 with the third most games in center field (1683) in National League history trailing only Willie Mays and Richie Ashburn.

Etta James (born Jamesetta Hawkins) January 25, 1938 - January 20, 2012

Singer who performed in various genres including blues, R&B, soul, rock and roll, jazz and gospel. Starting her career in 1954 she gained fame with hits such as The Wallflower, At Last, Tell Mama, Something's Got a Hold on Me and I'd Rather Go Blind. In total James won six Grammy Awards and 17 Blues Music Awards. She was inducted into the Rock and Roll Hall of Fame in 1993, the Blues Hall of Fame in 2001 and the Grammy Hall of Fame in both 1999 and 2008.

Judy Blume (born Judith Sussman) February 12, 1938

Writer whose best known works include Are You There God? It's Me, Margaret (1970), Tales of a Fourth Grade Nothing (1972), Deenie (1973) and Blubber (1974). Blume's books have sold over 82 million copies and have been translated into 32 languages. She was recognized as a Library of Congress Living Legend and she was awarded the 2004 National Book Foundation medal for distinguished contribution to American letters.

David Baltimore March 7, 1938

Biologist, university administrator and the 1975 Nobel laureate in Physiology or Medicine. He served as president of the California Institute of Technology (Caltech) from 1997 to 2006, and is currently the President Emeritus and Robert Andrews Millikan Professor of Biology at Caltech. Baltimore served as president of the American Association for the Advancement of Science in 2007 and received the U.S. National Medal of Science in 1999.

Janet Guthrie March 7, 1938

Retired professional race car driver and the first woman to qualify and compete in both the Indianapolis 500 and the Daytona 500. Guthrie was originally an aerospace engineer who started racing in 1963 on the SCCA circuit in a Jaguar XK 140 and by 1972 was racing full-time. She was one of the first elected to the International Women's Sports Hall of Fame and in 2006 was inducted into the International Motorsports Hall of Fame.

John Sherman 'Johnny' Rutherford III
March 12, 1938

Former automobile racer who is one of ten drivers to win the prestigious Indianapolis 500 mile race at least three times (1974, 1976 and 1980). Also known as 'Lone Star JR', he began racing modified stock cars in 1959 and he also dabbled in stock car racing (making 35 NASCAR Sprint Cup Series starts between 1963 and 1988). Rutherford was inducted in the Motorsports Hall of Fame of America in 1993.

Duane Eddy
April 26, 1938

Guitarist who in the late 1950s and early 1960s had a string of hit records produced by Lee Hazlewood which were noted for their characteristically twangy sound. These included recordings such as Rebel Rouser, Peter Gunn and Because They're Young. Eddy's records were equally as successful in the UK and by 1963 he had sold over 12 million records. He was inducted into the Rock and Roll Hall of Fame in 1994 and the Musicians Hall of Fame and Museum in 2008.

Jerry Alan West
May 28, 1938

Retired basketball player, manager and Olympic gold medalist who played his entire professional career for the Los Angeles Lakers. West's NBA career was highly successful being voted 12 times into the All-NBA First and Second Teams, and 14 times into the NBA All-Star Team. West holds the NBA record for the highest points per game average in a playoff series with 46.3 and is also the only player in NBA history to be a Finals MVP despite being on the losing team (1969).

Austin William 'Goose' Gonsoulin
June 7, 1938 -
September 8, 2014

Football player who played professionally as a safety in the American Football League for the Denver Broncos and in the National Football League for the San Francisco 49ers. At the end of his stint with the Broncos he was the AFL's all-time leader in interceptions with 40. Gonsoulin was a Sporting News AFL All-League player in 1960, 1962 and 1963, and an AFL Western Division All-Star in 1961, 1964 and 1966.

Joyce Carol Oates
June 16, 1938

Writer who published her first book in 1963 and has since published over 40 novels, as well as a number of plays and novellas, and many volumes of short stories, poetry and nonfiction. Oates has won a number of awards including the National Book Award, two O. Henry Awards and the National Humanities Medal. Her novels Black Water (1992), What I Lived For (1994), Blonde (2000) and short story collection Lovely, Dark, Deep: Stories (2014) were each finalists for the Pulitzer Prize.

William Harrison 'Bill' Withers, Jr.
July 4, 1938

Singer-songwriter and musician who performed and recorded from 1970 until 1985. He recorded several major hits, including Lean on Me, Ain't No Sunshine, Use Me, Just the Two of Us, Lovely Day, and Grandma's Hands. Withers has won three Grammy Awards during his career and has been nominated for four others. He was inducted into the West Virginia Music Hall of Fame in 2007 and the Rock and Roll Hall of Fame in 2015.

Brian Manion Dennehy
July 9, 1938

Actor of film, stage and television. He is the winner of one Golden Globe, two Tony Awards and the recipient of six Primetime Emmy Award nominations for his television movies. He gained initial recognition for his role as the antagonistic Sheriff Will Teasle in First Blood (1982). Some of his numerous roles in films include Gorky Park (1983), Silverado (1985), Cocoon (1985), F/X (1986), Romeo + Juliet (1996) and Knight of Cups (2015).

Natalie Wood (born Natalie Zacharenko)
July 20, 1938 -
November 28, 1981

Film and television actress who first worked in films as a child and became a successful Hollywood star as a young adult. Her best known screen roles include Miracle On 34th Street (1947), Rebel Without a Cause (1955), The Searchers (1956) and West Side Story (1961). By the time she was 25 years old she had received three Oscar nominations for her roles in the films Rebel Without a Cause, Splendor in the Grass (1961) and Love with the Proper Stranger (1963).

Janet Wood Reno
July 21, 1938 -
November 7, 2016

Former State Attorney who became the Attorney General of the United States from 1993 until 2001. She was nominated by President Bill Clinton on February 11, 1993, and confirmed on March 11, 1993. Reno became the first ever woman to serve as Attorney General and the second-longest serving Attorney General in U.S. history after William Wirt.

Kenneth Ray 'Kenny' Rogers
August 21, 1938

Singer, songwriter, actor, record producer and entrepreneur. Rogers has charted more than 120 hit singles across various music genres and topped the country and pop album charts for more than 200 individual weeks in the United States alone. Worldwide he has sold over 100 million records making him one of the best-selling music artists of all time. He was inducted into the Country Music Hall of Fame in 2013.

Elliott Gould (born Elliott Goldstein)
August 29, 1938

Actor who, in addition to his performance in Bob & Carol & Ted & Alice (1969) for which he received a nomination for the Academy Award for Best Supporting Actor, is perhaps best known for his leading roles in M*A*S*H (1970), The Long Goodbye (1973) and California Split (1974). More recently he has gained recognition for his supporting roles as Jack Geller on Friends (1994-2003), as Reuben Tishkoff in the Ocean's Trilogy (2001-2007) and as Ezra Goldman in Ray Donovan (2013-2015).

Gaylord Jackson Perry
September 15, 1938

Former Major League Baseball pitcher who played from 1962 to 1983 for eight different teams. During his 22-year baseball career Perry compiled 314 wins, 3,534 strikeouts and a 3.11 earned run average. Perry, a five-time All-Star, was the first pitcher to win the Cy Young Award in each league, winning it in the American League in 1972 with the Cleveland Indians and in the National League in 1978 with the San Diego Padres. He was elected to the Baseball Hall of Fame in 1991.

Benjamin Earl 'Ben E.' King
September 28, 1938 -
April 30, 2015

Record producer and Soul and R&B singer. He was perhaps best known as the singer and co-composer of 'Stand by Me' - a US Top 10 hit both in 1961 and later in 1986 (when it was used as the theme to the film of the same name). King was as one of the principal lead singers of the R&B vocal group the Drifters and notably sang the lead vocals on 'Save the Last Dance for Me', one of their biggest global hit singles.

Edward Raymond 'Eddie' Cochran
October 3, 1938 -
April 17, 1960

Musician whose rockabilly songs such as Twenty Flight Rock, Summertime Blues, C'mon Everybody and Somethin' Else captured teenage feelings in the mid to late 1950s. Cochran played the guitar, piano, bass and drums, and his image as a sharply dressed and good-looking young man with a rebellious attitude epitomized the stance of the 1950s rocker. In 1987, 27 years after his death at the age of 21, Cochran was inducted into the Rock and Roll Hall of Fame.

Robert Craig 'Evel' Knievel
October 17, 1938 -
November 30, 2007

Death-defying motorcycle performer whose series of spectacular airborne stunts in the 1960s and '70s brought him worldwide fame as the quintessential daredevil. Two of his most famous stunts included vaulting his motorcycle 151 feet over the fountains of Caesars Palace in Las Vegas and his 1974 attempt to jump across Snake River Canyon on a rocket-powered motorcycle. Knievel was inducted into the Motorcycle Hall of Fame in 1999.

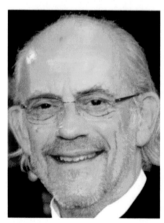

Christopher Allen Lloyd
October 22, 1938

Actor, voice actor and comedian best known for his roles as Doc Emmett Brown in the Back to the Future trilogy, Judge Doom in Who Framed Roger Rabbit (1988) and Uncle Fester in The Addams Family (1991) and its sequel Addams Family Values (1993). On television Lloyd has won two Primetime Emmy Awards for playing Jim Ignatowski in the comedy series Taxi (1978-1983) and earned a third Emmy for his 1992 guest appearance on Road to Avonlea.

Robert Edward 'Ted' Turner III
November 19, 1938

Media mogul and philanthropist. As a businessman he is known as founder of the Cable News Network (CNN) and WTBS. As a philanthropist he is known for his $1 billion gift to support the United Nations, which created the United Nations Foundation on which Turner serves as Chairman of the board of directors. Additionally in 2001 Turner co-founded the Nuclear Threat Initiative (NTI) with U.S. Senator Sam Nunn (D-GA).

Oscar Palmer Robertson
November 24, 1938

The 'Big O' is a retired NBA player who played for the Cincinnati Royals and Milwaukee Bucks. The 6ft 5in 205lb Robertson played point guard and was a 12-time All-Star, 11-time member of the All-NBA Team and one-time winner of the MVP award in 14 professional seasons. He is the only player in NBA history to average a triple-double for a season. In the 1970-71 season he was a key player in bringing the Bucks their only NBA title.

Connie Francis
(born Concetta Rosa Maria Franconero)
December 12, 1938

Pop singer and top-charting female vocalist who gained worldwide success when her father convinced her to record the decades-old tune Who's Sorry Now. Dick Clark introduced the song on his Bandstand TV show in 1958 and it became an immediate hit selling a million copies in less than six months. She then started working with songwriters Neil Sedaka and Howie Greenfield recording a string of hits including Stupid Cupid, Lipstick on Your Collar and Everybody's Somebody's Fool.

Jonathan Vincent 'Jon' Voight
December 29, 1938

Actor who has been nominated for 4 Academy Awards, winning one, and eleven Golden Globes, winning four. Voight came to prominence in the late 1960s with his performance in Midnight Cowboy (1969). During the 1970s he became a Hollywood star with his roles in Deliverance (1972), Coming Home (1978) and The Champ (1979), for which he won an Academy Award for Best Leading Actor. Voight is the father of actress Angelina Jolie and actor James Haven.

POPULAR MUSIC 1938

No.1   Artie Shaw   Begin The Beguine
No.2   The Andrews Sisters   Bei Mir Bist Du Schoen
No.3   Ella Fitzgerald   A-Tisket A-Tasket
No.4   The Seven Dwarfs   Whistle While You Work
No.5   Bob Hope & Shirley Ross   Thanks For The Memory
No.6   Fred Astaire   Change Partners
No.7   Bing Crosby & Connee Boswell   Alexander's Ragtime Band
No.8   Benny Goodman   Don't Be That Way
No.9   Bunny Berigan   I Can't Get Started
No.10   Bing Crosby   I've Got a Pocketful of
                                          Dreams

Artie Shaw And His Orchestra
Begin The Beguine

Label:	Written by:	Length:
Bluebird (B-7746)	Cole Porter	3 mins 16 secs

Artie Shaw (born Arthur Jacob Arshawsky; May 23, 1910 - December 30, 2004) was a clarinetist, composer, bandleader, author and actor. Widely regarded as one of jazz's finest clarinetists, Shaw led one of the most popular big bands of the late 1930s through the early 1940s. Though he had numerous hit records he was perhaps best known for this 1938 recording of Cole Porter's 'Begin The Beguine'.

 # The Andrews Sisters
Bei Mir Bist Du Schoen

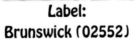

Label:	Written by:	Length:
Brunswick (02552)	Cahn / Chaplin / Secunda	3 mins 7 secs

The Andrews Sisters were a close harmony singing group from the eras of swing and boogie-woogie. The group consisted of three sisters: LaVerne Sophia (July 6, 1911 - May 8, 1967), Maxene Angelyn (January 3, 1916 - October 21, 1995) and Patricia Marie (February 16, 1918 - January 30, 2013). Throughout their long career the sisters sold well over 75 million records.

3 Ella Fitzgerald
A-Tisket A-Tasket

Label:
Decca (1840)

Written by:
Al Feldman / Ella Fitzgerald

Length:
2 mins 21 secs

Ella Jane Fitzgerald (April 25, 1917 - June 15, 1996) was a jazz singer often referred to as the Fi
Lady of Song, the Queen of Jazz and Lady Ella. 'A Tisket A Tasket' is a nursery rhyme th
Fitzgerald, in conjunction with Al Feldman, extended and embellished into a jazz piece. It was h
breakthrough hit with the Chick Webb Orchestra in 1938 and it has since become a jazz standard.

4 The Seven Dwarfs
Whistle While You Work

Label:
Bluebird (B-7343)

Written by:
Frank Churchill / Larry Morey

Length:
2 mins 42 secs

'Whistle While You Work' was written for the 1937 animated Disney film Snow White and the Sev
Dwarfs. It was performed by Shep Fields and his Rippling Rhythm Orchestra with vocal Refrain
Bobby Goday. In the film it was performed (unofficially) by voice actress Adriana Caselotti.

Bob Hope & Shirley Ross
Thanks For The Memory

Label:	Written by:	Length:
Decca (DLA 1583)	Leo Robin / Ralph Rainger	3 mins 8 secs

'**Thanks For The Memory**' was first introduced in the film The Big Broadcast Of 1938 by Harry Sosnik his Orchestra. With vocals by Bob Hope and Shirley Ross the song won the Academy Award for Best Original Song and became Hope's signature tune.

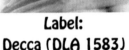 **Fred Astaire**
Change Partners

Label:	Written by:	Length:
Brunswick (8189)	Irving Berlin	3 mins 16 secs

Fred Astaire (May 10, 1899 - June 22, 1987) was a dancer, choreographer, singer, musician and actor. His stage and subsequent film and television careers spanned a total of 76 years. Change Partners was written by Irving Berlin for the 1938 film Carefree.

Bing Crosby & Connee Boswell
Alexander's Ragtime Band

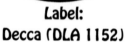

Label:
Decca (DLA 1152)

Written by:
Irving Berlin

Length:
2 mins 49 secs

'**Alexander's Ragtime Band**' was written by Irving Berlin and was his first major international hit 1911. The 1938 duet by Bing Crosby and Connee Boswell was recorded with the Victor You Orchestra in Los Angeles and coincided with the release of the film of the same name.

Benny Goodman
Don't Be That Way

Label:
RCA Victor (25792)

Written by:
Goodman / Sampson / Parish

Length:
3 mins 17 sec

Benjamin David 'Benny' Goodman (May 30, 1909 - June 13, 1986) was a jazz and swing musicia clarinetist and bandleader known as the 'King of Swing'. 'Don't Be That Way' was Goodmar opening number in his famous Carnegie Hall Concert on January 16, 1938, the first time a ja contingent had played the hallowed home of classical music. A month later he recorded it for RC Victor and it became a No.1 hit.

⑨ Bunny Berigan
I Can't Get Started

| Label: | Written by: | Length: |
| RCA Victor (EPA 5003) | Ira Gershwin / Vernon Duke | 4 mins 53 secs |

Roland Bernard 'Bunny' Berigan (November 2, 1908 - June 2, 1942) was a jazz trumpeter and bandleader who rose to fame during the swing era. He was best known for his virtuoso jazz trumpeting and this classic recording of 'I Can't Get Started' which was inducted into the Grammy Hall of Fame in 1975.

⑩ Bing Crosby
I've Got a Pocketful of Dreams

| Label: | Written by: | Length: |
| Decca (1933) | James V. Monaco / John Burke | 2 mins 35 secs |

Harry Lillis 'Bing' Crosby, Jr. (May 3, 1903 - October 14, 1977) was a singer and actor. Crosby's trademark warm bass-baritone voice made him the best-selling recording artist of the 20th century selling close to a billion records, tapes, compact discs and digital downloads worldwide.

TOP FILMS 1938

1. Alexander's Ragtime Band
2. Test Pilot
3. Boys Town
4. The Adventures Of Robin Hood
5. You Can't Take It with You

OSCARS

Best Film: You Can't Take It With You

Best Director: Frank Capra
(You Can't Take It With You)
Best Actor: Spencer Tracy
(Boys Town)
Best Actress: Bette Davis
(Jezebel)
Best Supporting Actor: Walter Brennan
(Kentucky)
Best Supporting Actress: Fay Bainter
(Jezebel)

Alexander's Ragtime Band

Directed by: Henry King - Runtime: 106 minutes

Roger Grant, a classical violinist, disappoints his family and teacher when he organizes a jazz band. Roger falls in love with his singer Stella but his reluctance to lose her leads him to thwart her efforts to become a solo star. When the World War separates them Stella marries Roger's best friend Charlie. Roger comes home after the war and an important concert at Carnegie Hall brings the corners of the romantic triangle together.

STARRING

Tyrone Edmund Power III
Born: May 5, 1914
Died: November 15, 1958

Character:
Alexander (Roger Grant)

Film, stage and radio actor. From the 1930s to the 1950s Power appeared in dozens of films, often in swashbuckler roles or romantic leads. His better-known films include The Mark Of Zorro (1940), The Black Swan (1942), Captain From Castile (1947), Prince Of Foxes (1949) and Witness For The Prosecution (1957). In 1960, 2 years after his death from a heart attack, he was honored with a star on the Hollywood Walk of Fame.

Alice Faye
Born: May 5, 1915
Died: May 9, 1998

Character:
Stella Kirby

Actress and singer who got her first major break in 1934 in the lead role in a film version of George White's '1935 Scandals'. She became a hit with film audiences and by 1939 Faye was named one of the top ten box office draws in Hollywood. She is often associated with the Academy Award–winning standard 'You'll Never Know' which she introduced in the musical film Hello, Frisco, Hello (1943).

Don Ameche
Born: May 31, 1908
Died: December 6, 1993

Character:
Charlie Dwyer

Actor and voice artist who after touring in vaudeville featured in many biographical films including The Story of Alexander Graham Bell (1939). He continued to appear on Broadway (as well as on radio and TV) where he was host and commentator for International Showtime covering circus and ice-shows all over Europe. Ameche went on to win the Academy Award for Best Supporting Actor for his performance in Cocoon (1985).

TRIVIA

Goofs

An on-location shot shows the Cliff House, a famous San Francisco restaurant, overlooking Ocean Beach. A 1930's model car drives by in the foreground however this scene takes place before World War I making the car about 20 years too early.

When Wally Vernon comes forward to do his specialty number he passes Alexander twice, glancing at him both times.

Interesting Facts

33 Irving Berlin compositions were initially used in the filming with only 3 not making the final cut.

CONTINUED

Interesting Facts   This was the first time that composer Irving Berlin had worked with Ethel Merman who plays Jerry Allen in the film. He told her that he was so impressed with her talent that he would work with her again. He kept that promise and wrote two Broadway shows especially for her: 'Annie Get Your Gun' in 1946 and 'Call Me Madam' in 1950, the latter of which also starred Merman in the film adaptation in 1953. Merman also later starred in a film that, like this one, was a cavalcade of Irving Berlin songs, There's No Business Like Show Business (1954).

20th Century Fox head Darryl F. Zanuck had this as one of his prestige productions of the year. The directing gig naturally went to his personal favorite choice, Henry King, who was always first choice for the studio's leading productions.

Irving Berlin balked at the idea of a biopic about him as he felt it would be too personally intrusive. Thus the idea to form a fictional story showcasing a large number of his songs was hatched.

Irving Berlin personally singled out Alice Faye to play the female lead.

Alexander's Ragtime Band earned the second highest number of Academy Award nominations for 1938 with six in total (behind You Can't Take It With You which had 7 nominations). Of the six nominations it went on to win just one Award which went to Alfred Newman for Best Original Score.

Quotes   **Stella Kirby:** You haven't left me with a word to say.
Charlie Dwyer: That's good. People talk too much anyway.

Sailor: So, did you ever learn long division?
Stella Kirby: I never even learned short division!

TEST PILOT

Directed by: Victor Fleming - Runtime: 119 minutes

Jim Lane is a test pilot whose professional life is dangerous and whose personal life compensates for that danger by fast living and recklessness.

STARRING

Clark Gable
Born: February 1, 1901
Died: November 16, 1960

Character:
Jim Lane

Actor often referred to as the 'King of Hollywood'. Gable began his career as a stage actor and appeared as an extra in silent films between 1924 and 1926. He progressed to supporting roles for MGM in 1931 and landed his first leading role soon after. Gable was a leading man in more than 60 motion pictures over the following three decades, winning an Oscar for Best Actor in It Happened One Night (1934).

Myrna Loy
Born: August 2, 1905
Died: December 14, 1993

Character:
Ann Thurston Barton

Film, television and stage actress who trained as a dancer. Although originally typecast in earlier films her career took off following her portrayal of Nora Charles in The Thin Man (1934). In March 1991 Loy was presented with an Honorary Academy Award with the inscription 'In recognition of her extraordinary qualities both on screen and off, with appreciation for a lifetime's worth of indelible performances.'

Spencer Tracy
Born: April 1, 1900
Died: June 10, 1967

Character:
Gunner Morse

Spencer Bonaventure Tracy was an actor noted for his natural style and versatility. One of the major stars of Hollywood's Golden Age Tracy appeared in 75 films and developed a reputation among his peers as one of the screen's greatest actors. Tracy was nominated for nine Academy Awards for Best Actor, winning two and sharing the record for total nominations with Laurence Olivier.

TRIVIA

Goofs

When Jim Lane and Gunner get in the B-17 and begin to taxi there are no numbers visible on either side of the nose. On starting the takeoff a large deformed S8 is painted on the left side of the nose - it is actually a reversed shot of the number 82. Two shots later the B-17 nose number then changes to a reversed 52. The subsequent shots in the air and during the crash depict the B-17 without numbers on the nose or tail. After Lane rejoins the Army Air Corp and he is lecturing the B-17 crew members, the fourth and fifth B-17's in line are numbered 52 and 82.

When the plane is going down in a Kansas field there are clearly mountains in the background. There are no mountains in Kansas.

CONTINUED

Interesting Facts The four engine bomber flown by Gable and Tracy near the end of the film was a Boeing Model 299B, Y1B-17 'Flying Fortress'. It was one of the 13 Y1B-17s acquired by the U.S. Army Air Corps for evaluation. The massed flight at the end of the film consisted of all 13 Y1B-17s that had been delivered by Boeing between January 11 and August 4, 1937. All were eventually redesignated B-17's.

Test Pilot is considered a significant aviation film by historians due to the use of contemporary aircraft.

The aircraft that Clark Gable took Myrna Loy up for her first flight was a Ryan Model ST-A. This plane actually belonged to John Gilbert 'Tex' Rankin who was an aerobatic pilot, air racer, barnstormer and flight instructor from the 1920s to the 1940s.

Test Pilot was claimed by Myrna Loy and Spencer Tracy as their personal favourite movie.

BOYS TOWN

Directed by: Norman Taurog - Runtime: 96 minutes

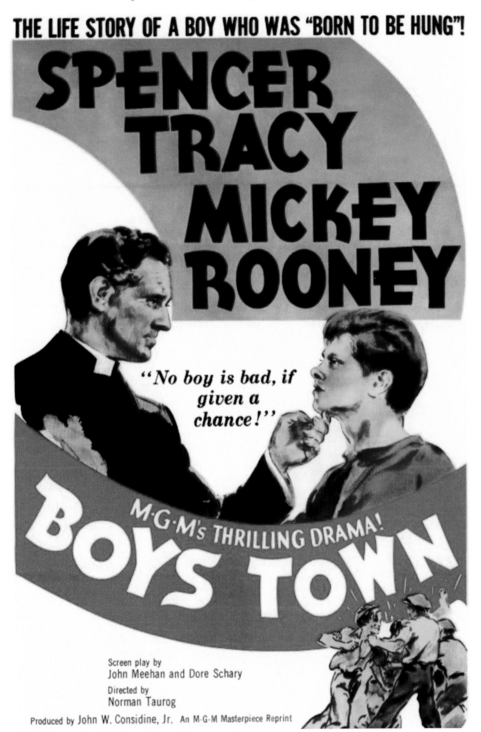

THE LIFE STORY OF A BOY WHO WAS "BORN TO BE HUNG"!

SPENCER TRACY
MICKEY ROONEY

"No boy is bad, if given a chance!"

M·G·M's THRILLING DRAMA!

BOYS TOWN

Screen play by
John Meehan and Dore Schary

Directed by
Norman Taurog

Produced by John W. Considine, Jr.   An M·G·M Masterpiece Reprint

Catholic Priest Father Flanagan, against all odds, opens Boys Town, a large orphanage for boys nobody wants. With love and the insistence that 'There is no such thing as a bad boy', he tries to get through to even the toughest kids.

STARRING

Spencer Tracy
Born: April 1, 1900
Died: June 10, 1967

Character:
Father Flanagan

Spencer Bonaventure Tracy was an actor noted for his natural style and versatility. One of the major stars of Hollywood's Golden Age Tracy appeared in 75 films and developed a reputation among his peers as one of the screen's greatest actors. Tracy was nominated for nine Academy Awards for Best Actor, winning two and sharing the record for total nominations with Laurence Olivier.

Mickey Rooney
Born: September 23, 1920
Died: April 6, 2014

Character:
Whitey Marsh

Actor of film, television, Broadway, radio and vaudeville. In a career spanning nine decades he appeared in more than 300 films and was one of the last surviving stars of the silent film era. Rooney was the top box office attraction from 1939 to 1941, and one of the best-paid actors of that era. During his career he received four Academy Award nominations and was nominated for five Emmy Awards, winning one.

Henry Watterson Hull
Born: October 3, 1890
Died: March 8, 1977

Character:
Dave Morris

Actor with a unique voice who is best remembered for playing the lead role in Universal Pictures' Werewolf Of London (1935). In total Hull appeared in 74 films between 1917 and 1966, often playing supporting characters such as the uncle of Tyrone Power's love interest Nancy Kelly in Jesse James (1939). Hull's last film was The Chase (1966) with Marlon Brando and Robert Redford.

TRIVIA

Goofs

While the boys are praying for the injured Pee Wee, Whitey goes behind them and grabs a branch of a tree with no leaves. When he turns around the branch is covered with leaves.

Interesting Facts

The day after Spencer Tracy won the Best Actor Oscar for his performance in this film, an MGM publicist released a statement - without consulting Tracy first - that the actor would donate his Oscar to the real Boys Town in Nebraska. Tracy agreed to make the donation if the Academy would send him a replacement Oscar. When the replacement arrived the engraving on the award read: "Best Actor - Dick Tracy."

CONTINUED

Interesting Facts   When shooting began on the movie Mickey Rooney repeatedly tried to steal scenes by fumbling with a handkerchief and pulling faces amongst other things. This so annoyed Spencer Tracy that he threatened to have Rooney thrown off the movie unless he behaved.

Freddie Bartholomew was considered for the part of Mickey Rooney's best friend but was not cast because the producers felt he was too associated with Little Lord Fauntleroy (1936), and that he would not be believable in this film.

Father Edward Flanagan, who died almost ten years after this movie was released, was the first person ever to live to see somebody win an Oscar for portraying him.

Father Flanagan was paid $5000 for the movie rights to his book; the movie made a profit of $2 million.

"I didn't go up to take him out...that's why it happened!"

THE ADVENTURES OF ROBIN HOOD

Directed by: Michael Curtiz & William Keighley - Runtime: 102 minutes

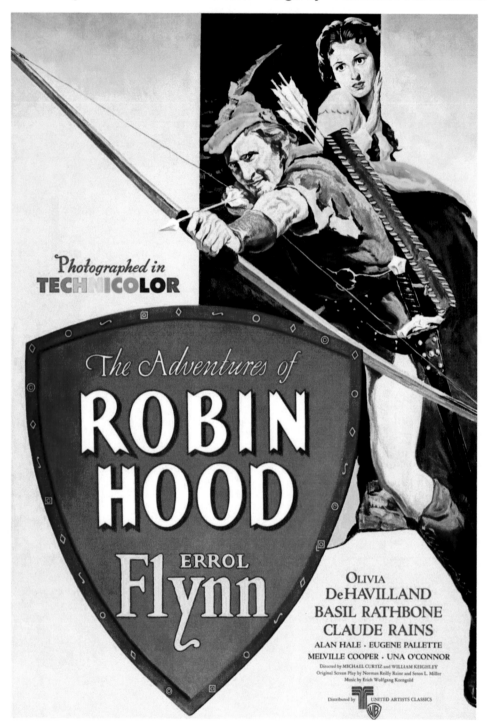

Sir Robin of Locksley runs afoul of Norman authority and is forced to turn outlaw. With his band of Merry Men he robs from the rich gives to the poor whilst trying to foil the cruel Sir Guy of Gisbourne, keep the nefarious Prince John off the throne and woo the lovely Maid Marian.

STARRING

Errol Leslie Flynn
Born: June 20, 1909
Died: October 14, 1959

Character:
Robin Hood

Australian-born actor who achieved fame in his first Hollywood role as Peter Blood in Captain Blood (1935). He was known for his romantic swashbuckler roles in Hollywood films as well as his frequent partnerships with Olivia De Havilland (8 films in total). In 1940, at the zenith of his career, Flynn was voted the fourteenth most popular star in the US and the seventh most popular in Britain. Flynn became an American citizen in 1942.

Olivia Mary de Havilland
Born: July 1, 1916

Character:
Maid Marian

British-American actress whose career spanned from 1935 to 1990. She appeared in 49 feature films and was one of the leading movie stars during the golden age of Classical Hollywood. She is best known for her early screen performances in The Adventures of Robin Hood (1938) and Gone with the Wind (1939), and her later award-winning performances in To Each His Own (1946), The Snake Pit (1948) and The Heiress (1949).

Philip St. John Basil Rathbone
Born: June 13, 1892
Died: July 21, 1967

Character:
Sir Guy of Gisbourne

South African-born English actor who rose to prominence in the United Kingdom as a Shakespearean stage actor and went on to appear in more than 70 films, primarily costume dramas, swashbucklers and the occasional horror film. His most famous role was that of Sherlock Holmes in fourteen Hollywood films made between 1939 and 1946. Rathbone was nominated for two Academy Awards and won three stars on the Hollywood Walk of Fame.

TRIVIA

Goofs

A car can be seen in the background when Will Scarlet gets off his horse to go to the aid of Much.

In the fight scene between Robin and Little John on the log, Will Scarlett begins to play what appears to be a stringless mandolin.

During the final fight scene between Robin Hood and Guy of Gisbourne, Guy knocks Robin over with a table and the leg of the table breaks off. In the next shot, when Robin kicks the table at Guy, the leg has re-attached itself.

Interesting Facts   During one fight sequence Errol Flynn was jabbed by an actor who was using an unprotected sword. After asking him why he didn't have a guard on the point the other actor apologized and explained that director Michael Curtiz had instructed him to remove the safety feature in order to make the action 'more exciting'. Flynn reportedly climbed up a gantry where Curtiz was standing next to the camera, took him by the throat and then asked him if he found that 'exciting enough'.

While filming Robin Hood's escape from the castle Basil Rathbone was knocked down and trampled by extras causing a spear wound in his right foot that required eight stitches to close.

This film production used all 11 of the Technicolor cameras in existence in 1938. At the end of each day's filming they were all returned to Technicolor.

Although shot in California, indigenous English plants were added and the grass was painted to give a greener, more English look.

At the time of its release this was Warners' most expensive film, costing over $2 million.

Douglas Fairbanks Jr. turned down the role of Robin Hood because he didn't want to be viewed as aping his father Douglas Fairbanks's starring role in Robin Hood (1922).

Quotes   **Lady Marian Fitzswalter:** Why, you speak treason!
Robin Hood: Fluently.

Little John: It'll take all the deer in Sherwood Forest to fill that belly!
Friar Tuck: And twice that to fill your empty head!

Sir Guy of Gisbourne: What the devil?
Robin Hood: Come now, Sir Guy. You would not kill a man for telling the truth, would you?
Sir Guy of Gisbourne: If it amused me, yes!

You Can't Take It With You

Directed by: Frank Capra - Runtime: 126 minutes

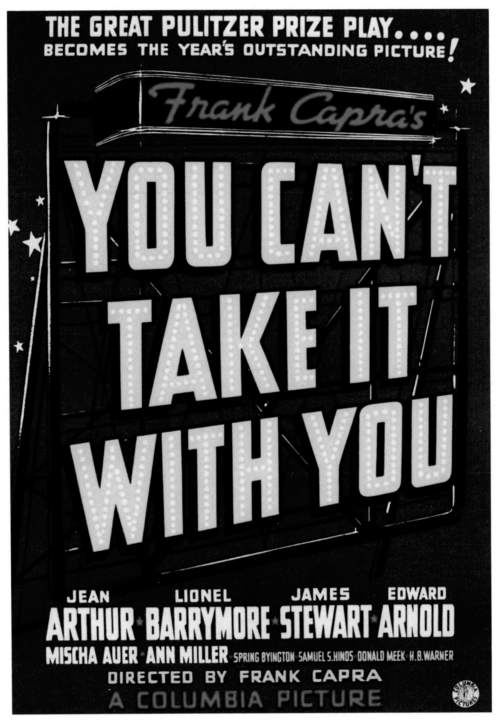

Alice Sycamore has to introduce the family of her fiancé, Tony Kirby, to her own family. The Kirby's are a wealthy, stuffy family of great self- importance, while the Sycamore's are a collection of good-hearted lunatics. When the two families come together, lifestyle and philosophy collide head-on.

STARRING

Jean Arthur
Born: October 17, 1900
Died: June 19, 1991

Character:
Alice Sycamore

Actress and a major film star of the 1930s and 1940s. Arthur had feature roles in three Frank Capra films: Mr Deeds Goes to Town (1936), You Can't Take It With You (1938), and Mr Smith Goes to Washington (1939), films that championed the 'everyday heroine'. Arthur was nominated for an Academy Award for Best Actress in 1944 for her performance in The More the Merrier (1943) and has been called 'the quintessential comedic leading lady'.

Lionel Barrymore
Born: April 28, 1878
Died: November 15, 1954

Character:
Martin Vanderhof

Actor of stage, screen and radio as well as a film director. He won an Academy Award for Best Actor for his performance in A Free Soul (1931) but remains perhaps best known for the role of the villainous Mr Potter character in Frank Capra's film It's a Wonderful Life (1946). He has two stars on the Hollywood Walk of Fame and is also a member of the American Theatre Hall of Fame along with his siblings Ethel and John.

James Maitland Stewart
Born: May 20, 1908
Died: July 2, 1997

Character:
Tony Kirby

Actor and military officer who is among the most honoured and popular stars in film history. Stewart was nominated for five Academy Awards, winning one for The Philadelphia Story (1940) and receiving a Lifetime Achievement award in 1985. He also had a noted military career and was a World War II and Vietnam War veteran who rose to the rank of Brigadier General in the U.S. Air Force Reserve (becoming the highest-ranking actor in military history).

TRIVIA

Goofs

When Tony hands Alice a yellow rose in the office she holds it upright in front of her. In the next shot it's lying across her lap; in the next it's upright again.

When Alice is in the courtroom scene she is wearing a trench coat as newspaper photographers take pictures. When we see the newspaper pictures she is not wearing the coat.

Interesting Facts

Shortly before filming began Lionel Barrymore lost the use of his legs to crippling arthritis and a hip injury. To accommodate him the script was altered so that his character had a sprained ankle and he did the film on crutches.

Interesting Facts Frank Capra was President of the Academy of Motion Picture Arts and Sciences in 1938 and was at the forefront of a union dispute amongst producers and directors that were threatening to disrupt that year's Oscar ceremony. Fortunately it was resolved in time for the President to walk off with 2 more Oscars to add to his collection.

Lionel Barrymore plays Jean Arthur's grandfather in the film. In reality he was only 22 years her senior.

A 1938 feature film usually ran to 8,000 feet of film. Frank Capra shot 329,000 feet for this one.

Shooting began in late April 1938 and took just under 2 months. The cost came in at one and a half million dollars.

Ann Miller was only 15 years old when this movie was filmed. Her character is called on to perform numerous (amateur) ballet positions including the toe pointe which was very painful for her. She hid this from the cast and crew but would cry (out of sight) off stage. James Stewart noticed her crying (though he didn't know why) and would have boxes of candy to make her feel better.

The original play by Moss Hart and George S. Kaufman won the 1937 Pulitzer Prize for Drama and was still running on Broadway when the film opened.

Columbia paid $200,000 for the film rights to the play.

Quotes **Grandpa Martin Vanderhoff:** Maybe it'd stop you trying to be so desperate about making more money than you can ever use? You can't take it with you, Mr. Kirby. So what good is it? As near as I can see the only thing you can take with you is the love of your friends.

Grandpa Martin Vanderhof: Lincoln said, 'With malice toward none, with charity to all.' Nowadays they say, 'Think the way I do or I'll bomb the daylights outta you.'

Sporting Winners

Don Budge - Tennis

Associated Press - Male Athlete of the Year

John Donald 'Don' Budge
Born: June 13, 1915 in Oakland, California
Died: January 26, 2000 in Scranton, Pennsylvania

Don Budge was an American tennis champion who was a World No.1 player first as an amateur and then as a professional. He is most famous as the first ever player (and only American male) to win all four Grand Slam tournaments in the same year. He was also only the second male player to win all four Grand Slams after Fred Perry and is still the youngest to achieve that feat. In total Budge won a total of 14 Grand Slam tournaments (including a record 6 consecutive Grand Slam singles titles) and 4 Pro Slams, the latter achieved on three different surfaces. Budge was considered to have one of the best backhands in the history of tennis.

Grand Slam Titles:

	Singles	Doubles	Mixed Doubles
Australian Open	1938	-	-
French Open	1938	-	-
Wimbledon	1937 / 1938	1937 / 1938	1937 / 1938
U.S. Open	1937 / 1938	1936 / 1938	1937 / 1938

In 1942 Budge joined the United States Army Air Force to serve in World War II. After the war Budge played for a few years recording his last significant victory in 1954 in a North American tour beating Pancho Gonzales (by then the best player in the world). After retiring from competition Budge coached and conducted tennis clinics for children and was inducted into the International Tennis Hall of Fame at Newport, Rhode Island in 1964.

PATTY BERG - GOLF

ASSOCIATED PRESS - FEMALE ATHLETE OF THE YEAR

Patricia Jane Berg
Born: February 13, 1918 in Minneapolis, Minnesota
Died: September 10, 2006 in Fort Myers, Florida

Patricia Jane Berg was a professional golfer and a founding member (and then leading player) on the LPGA Tour during the 1940s, 1950s and 1960s. Her 15 major title wins remain the all-time record for most major wins by a female golfer.

LPGA major championship wins:

Western Open	1941	1943	1948	1951	1955	1957	1958
Titleholders Championship	1937	1938	1939	1948	1953	1955	1957
U.S. Women's Open	1946						

LPGA Vare Trophy: 1953, 1955 and 1956

In 1934, aged 16, Berg she decided to take up the sport of golf and not only did she begin her amateur career that year but also won her first title. Over the next six years Berg would gain national fame and win 29 amateur titles. She turned pro in 1940 but with the advent of the United States entering World War II in 1942, Patty Berg, one of the best female golfers in the world, laid down her clubs and joined the United States Marines Corps. After basic training and officer candidate school, Berg was commissioned a second lieutenant. Though not the job she chose her main duty was to promote military recruiting. Berg would serve her country from 1942-45 and after her discharge from the Corps she resumed her golf career. Berg's career would be one of the most stellar and influential in the history of women's sports. She won a total of 63 professional titles and was inducted into the World's Golf Hall of Fame in 1951. She was also the winner of the Associated Press Female Athlete Of The Year not only in 1938 but also in 1943 and 1955 as well, and was the LPGA Tour Money Winner in 1954, 1955 and 1957.

GOLF

THE MASTERS - HENRY PICARD

The Masters Tournament is the first of the majors to be played each year and unlike the other major championships it is played at the same location - Augusta National Golf Club, Georgia. This was the 5th Masters Tournament and was held April 2-4. Henry Picard led by one stroke after 54 holes and shot 70 in the final round to win his only Masters. The total prize fund was $5,000 with Picard taking home $1,500.

U.S. OPEN - RALPH GULDAHL

The U.S. Open Championship (established in 1895) was held June 9-11 at Cherry Hills Country Club in Englewood, Colorado, a suburb south of Denver. Defending champion Ralph Guldahl won his second straight U.S. Open title six strokes ahead of runner-up Dick Metz. His six-shot victory was the largest since Jim Barnes won by nine strokes in 1921 and was the second of Guldahl's three major titles. This was the first U.S. Open in which the players were limited to a maximum of 14 clubs; the USGA rule (4-4) went into effect in January 1938 (Guldahl won the title in 1937 with 19 clubs in his bag).

PGA CHAMPIONSHIP - PAUL RUNYAN

The 1938 and 21st PGA Championship was played July 10-16 at Shawnee Country Club in Smithfield Township, Pennsylvania. Then a match play championship, Paul Runyan won his second PGA Championship defeating the favored Sam Snead 8 & 7. Runyan was five holes up after the morning round then needed just eleven holes to finish off Snead (the largest victory margin ever in the match play finals of the PGA Championship). The total prize fund was $10,000 and the winner's share was $1,100.

Henry Picard

Ralph Guldahl

Paul Runyan

WORLD SERIES - NEW YORK YANKEES

New York Yankees 4 - 0 **Chicago Cubs**

Total attendance: 200,833 - Average attendance: 50,208
Winning player's share: $5,729 - Losing player's share: $4,675

The World Series is the annual championship series of Major League Baseball. Played since 1903 between the American League (AL) champion team and the National League (NL) champion, it is determined through a best-of-seven playoff.

The 1938 World Series matched the two-time defending champions the New York Yankees against the Chicago Cubs. The Yankees won in four games for their third championship in a row and their seventh in fifteen years. They would go on to make it four in a row in 1939 and eventually managed five in a row from 1949 to 1953. After Game 2 of the Series the Bronx Bombers would not return to Wrigley Field for nearly 65 years until a three-game interleague series with the Cubs beginning June 6, 2003.

	Date	Score	Location	Time	Att.
1	Oct 5	**New York Yankees - 3** Chicago Cubs - 1	Wrigley Field	1:53	43,642
2	Oct 6	**New York Yankees - 6** Chicago Cubs - 3	Wrigley Field	1:53	42,108
3	Oct 8	Chicago Cubs - 2 **New York Yankees - 5**	Yankee Stadium	1:57	55,236
4	Oct 9	Chicago Cubs - 3 **New York Yankees - 8**	Yankee Stadium	2:11	59,847

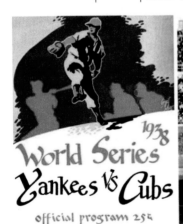

Sore-armed Dizzy Dean, left, of the Chicago Cubs battles Joe DiMaggio.

Horse Racing

Jockey George Woolf with Seabiscuit.

Seabiscuit (May 23, 1933 - May 17, 1947) was a champion Thoroughbred racehorse who was named Horse of the Year in 1938. On November 1, 1938, Seabiscuit met War Admiral in what was dubbed the 'Match of the Century'. The event was run at Pimlico Race Course and the estimated 40,000 at the track were joined by 40 million listening on the radio. War Admiral was the favorite but Seabiscuit pulled away to extend his lead over the closing stretch and finally win the race by four lengths. In 1958 Seabiscuit was voted into the National Museum of Racing and Hall of Fame.

Kentucky Derby - Lawrin

The Kentucky Derby is held annually at Churchill Downs in Louisville, Kentucky on the first Saturday in May. The race is a Grade 1 stakes race for three-year-olds and is one and a quarter miles in length.

Preakness Stakes - Dauber

The Preakness Stakes is held on the third Saturday in May each year at Pimlico Race Course in Baltimore, Maryland. It is a Grade 1 race run over a distance of 9.5 furlongs (1 3/16 miles) on dirt.

Belmont Stakes - Pasteurized

The Belmont Stakes is Grade 1 race held every June at Belmont Park in Elmont, New York. It is 1.5 miles in length and open to three-year-old thoroughbreds. It takes place on a Saturday between June 5 and June 11.

FOOTBALL - NFL CHAMPIONSHIP

CHAMPIONSHIP GAME

New York Giants　　23 - 17　　**Green Bay Packers**

Played: December 11, 1938 at the Polo Grounds in New York City.
Attendance: 48,120

The 1938 NFL season was the 19th regular season of the National Football League. The season ended when the New York Giants defeated the Green Bay Packers 23-17 in the NFL Championship Game.

Division Results:

Eastern Division

Team	P	W	L	T	PCT	PF	PA
New York Giants	**11**	**8**	**2**	**1**	**.800**	**194**	**79**
Washington Redskins	11	6	3	2	.667	148	154
Brooklyn Dodgers	11	4	4	3	.500	131	161
Philadelphia Eagles	11	5	6	0	.455	154	164
Pittsburgh Pirates	11	2	9	0	.182	79	169

Western Division

Team	P	W	L	T	PCT	PF	PA
Green Bay Packers	**11**	**8**	**3**	**0**	**.727**	**233**	**118**
Detroit Lions	11	7	4	0	.636	119	108
Chicago Bears	11	6	5	0	.545	194	148
Cleveland Rams	11	4	7	0	.364	131	215
Chicago Cardinals	11	2	9	0	.182	111	168

P= Games Played, W = Wins, L = Losses, T = Ties,
PCT= Winning Percentage, PF= Points For, PA = Points Against
Note: The NFL did not officially count tie games in the standings until 1972.

League Leaders

Statistic	Name	Team	Yards
Passing	Ace Parker	Brooklyn Dodgers	865
Rushing	Whizzer White	Pittsburgh Pirates	567
Receiving	Don Hutson	Green Bay Packers	548

HOCKEY: 1937-38 NHL SEASON

The 1937-38 NHL season was the 21st season of the National Hockey League with eight teams each playing 48 games. The Chicago Black Hawks were the Stanley Cup winners beating the Toronto Maple Leafs three games to one in the final series to take the Cup for the second time.

Final Standings:

	American Division	GP	W	L	T	GF	GA	Pts
1	**Boston Bruins**	48	30	11	7	142	89	67
2	New York Rangers	48	27	15	6	149	96	60
3	Chicago Black Hawks	48	14	25	9	97	139	37
4	Detroit Red Wings	48	12	25	11	99	133	35

	Canadian Division	GP	W	L	T	GF	GA	Pts
1	**Toronto Maple Leafs**	48	24	15	9	151	127	57
2	New York Americans	48	19	18	11	110	111	49
3	Montreal Canadiens	48	18	17	13	123	128	49
4	Montreal Maroons	48	12	30	6	101	149	30

Scoring Leaders:

	Player	Team	Goals	Assists	Points
1	**Gordie Drillon**	**Toronto Maple Leafs**	26	26	52
2	Syl Apps	Toronto Maple Leafs	21	29	50
3	Paul Thompson	Chicago Black Hawks	22	22	44

Hart Trophy (Most Valuable Player): Eddie Shore - Boston Bruins
Vezina Trophy (Fewest Goals Allowed): Tiny Thompson - Boston Bruins

STANLEY CUP

Chicago Black Hawks

3 - 1

Toronto Maple Leafs

Series Summary:

	Date	Home Team	Result	Road Team
1	April 5	**Chicago Black Hawks**	3-1	Toronto Maple Leafs
2	April 7	Chicago Black Hawks	1-5	**Toronto Maple Leafs**
3	April 10	Toronto Maple Leafs	1-2	**Chicago Black Hawks**
4	April 12	Toronto Maple Leafs	1-4	**Chicago Black Hawks**

INDIANAPOLIS 500 - FLOYD ROBERTS

The 26th International 500-Mile Sweepstakes Race was held at the Indianapolis Motor Speedway on Monday, May 30, 1938. The race was won by the number 23 car driven by Floyd Roberts. Roberts' car started in pole position and was the first car to win from that start since 1930. Roberts led 92 laps, posted an average (record) speed of 117.2mph and won $32,075. Roberts' car was owned by Lou Moore who was also the chief mechanic. The race was marred by the death of 33-year-old spectator Everett Spence. On lap 45 the number 42 car driven by Emil Andres hit the wall in turn two then flipped over several times causing its right front wheel to fly off. The wheel traveled 100 feet through the air and hit Spence who was pronounced dead upon arriving at the hospital. Andres suffered a concussion, broken nose, and chest injuries. The following year Floyd Roberts, driving the same car, was killed in a crash on the backstretch after hitting a wooden fence at 100mph. Roberts was the first former winner and defending champion of the race to have been killed while competing. According to reports Roberts had intended to retire following the race.

BOSTON MARATHON
LESLIE PAWSON

The Boston Marathon is the oldest annual marathon in the world and dates back to 1897.

Race result:

1.	**Leslie Pawson (USA)**	**2:35:34**
2.	Pat Dengis (USA)	2:36:41
3.	John A. Kelley (USA)	2:37:34

Mens Singles Champion - Don Budge - United States
Ladies Singles Champion - Alice Marble - United States

The 1938 U.S. National Championships (now known as the U.S. Open) took place on the outdoor grass courts at the West Side Tennis Club, Forest Hills in New York. The tournament ran from September 8-24. It was the 58th staging of the U.S. National Championships and the fourth Grand Slam tennis event of the year.

Men's Singles Final:

Country	Player	Set 1	Set 2	Set 3	Set 4
United States	Don Budge	6	6	6	6
United States	Gene Mako	3	8	2	1

Women's Singles Final:

Country	Player	Set 1	Set 2
United States	Alice Marble	6	6
Australia	Nancye Wynne Bolton	0	3

Men's Doubles Final:

Country	Players	Set 1	Set 2	Set 3
United States	Don Budge / Gene Mako	6	6	6
Australia	Adrian Quist / John Bromwich	3	2	1

Women's Doubles Final:

Country	Players	Set 1	Set 2	Set 3
United States	Sarah Palfrey Cooke / Alice Marble	6	6	6
France / Poland	Simonne Mathieu / Jadwiga Jędrzejowska	8	4	3

Mixed Doubles Final:

Country	Players	Set 1	Set 2
United States	Alice Marble / Don Budge	6	6
Australia	Thelma Coyne Long / John Bromwich	1	2

THE COST OF LIVING

Delicious and Refreshing

ICE-COLD Coca-Cola

DRINK Coca-Cola

It's part of the game to take "time-out" for ice-cold Coca-Cola . . . adding to relaxation what relaxation always needs, — pure, wholesome refreshment.

THE PAUSE THAT REFRESHES

COMPARISON CHART

	1938	1938 Price Today (Including Inflation)	2017	Real Term % Change
House	$9,100	$156,726	$290,400	+85.3%
Annual Income	$1,060	$18,256	$54,920	+200.8%
Car	$1,375	$23,681	$32,994	+39.3%
Gallon of Gasoline	15¢	$2.58	$2.32	-10.1%
Gallon of Milk	18¢	$3.10	$4.04	+30.3%
DC Comic Book	10¢	$1.72	$3.99	+132.0%

GROCERIES

A-Y White Bread Loaf (24oz)	9¢
Safeway Butter (per lb)	25¢
Fresh Country Eggs (2 dozen)	25¢
Max-i-mum Milk (3 tall cans)	19¢
Carnation Milk (4 small cans)	15¢
Granulated Sugar (10lb bag)	48¢
Peerless Flour (48 pounds)	$1.29¢
Pure Hog Lard (per lb)	10¢
Shredded Wheat (pkg.)	12¢
Kellogg's Corn Flakes (2 boxes)	13¢
Full Cream Cheese (per lb)	19¢
Fresh Apple Pies (each)	15¢
Donuts (each)	1¢
Blue Diamond Popcorn (2lb bag)	19¢
Peanut Butter (quart jar)	21¢
Bananas (per lb)	4¢
California Oranges (per dozen)	13¢
Apples (per dozen)	10¢
Lemons (per dozen)	23¢
Del Monte Sliced Pineapple (3x No.1 cans)	25¢
Home Grown Tomatoes (per lb)	6¢
Tomatoes (12x No.2 cans)	48¢
Hard Head Lettuce (each)	4¢
Potatoes No.1 Rurals (10lb)	15¢
Cabbage (2lbs)	5¢
Green Beans (per lb)	10¢
Carrots (2 bunches)	5¢
Corn (3x No.2 cans)	23¢
Pork Sausage (per lb)	10¢
Hamburgers (each)	5¢
Sliced Cured Ham (per lb)	25¢
Steak (per lb)	25¢
Leg 'O Lamb (per lb)	22¢
Fresh Calf Brains (per lb)	15¢
Full Dressed Hens (per lb)	22¢
Large Size Oysters (pt.)	29¢
Sunnyfield Sliced Bacon (per lb)	33¢
Meat Loaf (per lb)	12½¢
Campbell's Pork And Beans (can)	7¢
Heinz Spaghetti (2 large cans)	25¢
Heinz Ketchup (14oz bottle)	19¢
Jello (any flavor pkg.)	5¢
Maxwell House Coffee (per lb)	26¢
8 O'Clock Coffee (3lb bag)	43¢
Lipton's Tea (¼lb pkg.)	21¢
Stokely's Tomato Juice (14oz can)	5¢
Lifebuoy Soap (2 bars)	15¢
Waldorf Tissue Paper (6 rolls)	22¢

CLOTHES

Women's Clothing

Squirrel Locks Fur Coat	$115
Jiggers Tweedy Woolen Coat	$10.95
J.M. Dyer Two Piece Casual Suit	$7.95
Marks Bros. Spring Frock	$7.95
Sears Built-Up Denim Slacks	89¢
Satin Seraphim Pyjamas	$4.95
Shelby Pure Silk Slip	$2.25
Vanity Fair Pechglo Panties	$1
Miramar Black Patent Shoes	$8.95
Kinney's Pure Silk Stockings (3 pairs)	$2

Men's Clothing

Kuppenheimer Valgora Coat	$38
Stetson's Playboy Hat	$5
Marks Bros. Straw Hat	98¢
Gabardine Double Breasted Spring Suit	$19.50
Sanforized Oxhide Overalls	69¢
Manhattan Shirt	$1.65
Ardsley Challis Tie	59¢
Blue Twill Khaki Work Pants	79¢
Horner Tailored Pyjamas	$1.65
J.M Dyer Standish Shoes	$5.95
Arrow Handkerchiefs	25¢

BOLERO & SASH
88¢
[A]
ACETATE RAYON CREPE

"MEXICANA" – nubby knit
today's $1.29 quality
97¢
[E]

BOLERO & SLACKS
97¢
[B]

BLOUSE & SLACKS
$1.98
[C]

"FIESTA" – rayon crepe blouse
$1.29 quality
97¢
[D]

"GAY CABALLERO"
acetate rayon blouse
97¢
[F]

TOYS

2-Speed Twin Bar Elgin Bicycle	$28.95
Streamliner Pedal Car	$9.69
Half-Oval Fiber Doll Buggy	$4.98
Sears 41in Fleet Arrow Sled	$3.48
Flirty Eye Teddy Bear	$1.59
Donald & Mickey Tea Set	48¢
Two-Gun Pete Novelty Suit	$2.49
Marx G-Man Tommy Gun	94¢
Buck Jones Air Rifle	$3.25
Toy Cash Register	89¢
Lionel Remote Control Electric Train Set	$9.95
Baseball Bat, Glove & Ball	69¢
Sears 57 Piece Stock Farm Set	59¢
Betsy Wetsy 11in Doll	$2.98
Wollensak Micro-Telescope	$1.59
DeVoe Water Color Paint Set	39¢

OTHER ITEMS

Oldsmobile 'Sixty', Four Door Sedan	$889
Tekell Sofa And Chair	$89.50
Dining Room Suite Inc. Table, Six Chairs & China Cabinet	$79.50
Wizard Electric Washer & Wringer	$49.95
Silvertone 10 Tube Performance Radio	$33.45
Kenmore Vacuum Cleaner	$23.95
Champion Electric Dry Shaver	$9.89
Sears Finest Coach Stroller	$24.50
72in Artificial Christmas tree	$3.89
7 Diamond Engagement Ring	$42.85
Elizabeth Arden Night And Day Eau De Toilette	$4.50
Sears Supertone Amplifying Guitar	$12.95
Ingraham Mantel Clock	$8.95
Remington Portable Typewriter	$39.75

U.S. COINS

Official Circulated U.S. Coins		Years Produced
Half-Cent	½¢	1792 - 1857
Cent (Penny)	1¢	1793 - Present
2-Cent	2¢	1864 - 1873
3-Cent	3¢	1851 - 1889
Half-Dime	5¢	1792 - 1873
Five Cent Nickel	5¢	1866 - Present
Dime	10¢	1792 - Present
20-Cent	20¢	1875 - 1878
Quarter	25¢	1796 - Present
Half Dollar	50¢	1794 - Present
Dollar Coin	$1	1794 - Present
Quarter Eagle	$2.50	1792 - 1929
Three-Dollar Piece	$3	1854 - 1889
Four-Dollar Piece	$4	1879 - 1880
Half Eagle	$5	1795 – 1929
Commemorative Half Eagle	$5	1980 - Present
Silver Eagle	$1	1986 - Present
Gold Eagle	$5	1986 - Present
Platinum Eagle	$10 - $100	1997 - Present
Double Eagle (Gold)	$20	1849 - 1933
Half Union	$50	1915

**Get the Facts on De Soto's VALUE and ECONOMY—
See How this Great Car Saves You Money Two Ways!**

Made in the USA
Middletown, DE
21 March 2019